Can It Really Be That Simple?

Can It Really Be That Simple?

Change Your Energy
Change Your World

TRISH DOODY

MEDIA NOX
PUBLISHING

ORLANDO, FLORIDA, USA

Media Nox Publishing
Orlando, Florida
Copyright © 2024 by Tricia Doody. All rights reserved.
Library of Congress Control Number: 2024920137
Paperback ISBN: 9798218503512
eBook ISBN: 9798218503529

Book cover design by Christina Thiele
Interior design by Christina Thiele
Editorial production by KN Literary Arts

This book is dedicated to YOU, the reader, for being open to possibilities. And to my beloved horse Midnight, whose patience and perseverance transformed my world and reminded me what this journey is all about.

Deepest gratitude to all my mentors, both human and horses, who have guided me on this journey and shared their amazing gifts. Forever in my heart.

Contents

Introduction

Over the years, I have found that people—be it family, friends, acquaintances, or even strangers—were drawn to me to seek advice. After a brief discussion, they would leave feeling uplifted, like they were suddenly on a clearer path. At the time, I didn't realize what I was actually doing, and it always baffled me why something so obvious and simple to me would not be obvious to them.

Fast forward many years and many, many enlightening experiences and discoveries later, I realized that what I was actually doing was working with energy. I could easily feel and read the energy that people were putting out but hiding behind, and I was able to help them by interpreting their own energy back to them. Simply put, I was telling them what they already knew internally but were blocking from themselves. Even more interesting is that my ability to feel energy is not limited to being near someone physically. I can immediately feel the energy of a person from a text or email, even if I've never met them. This shows you how powerful energy is.

I went from unknowingly using energy to realizing what it is and the power of using it when horses came into my life. Horses are masters of energy and amazing teachers. They gave me the magical gift of being able to change my energy—and ultimately my world—by simply becoming aware of it. This precious gift turned my life around, and now I want to share that gift with you. Throughout this book, I'll share my experiences with horses to illustrate how energy works, but these lessons are not unique to horses. You can apply them to everyone: humans, animals, and all living creatures.

As I've evolved on my journey and learned more about how energy works, I've realized that I am able to help people from all walks of life, regardless of their age, gender, or background, by reading their energy, often in just a brief encounter or conversation. Looking at it a bit more intensely, I realized that, in these encounters, I share consistent explanations about how their energy works, how powerful that is, and multiple examples of things I've learned along the way.

It finally hit me that if I can help random people I meet in my everyday life, maybe if I took the time to write down the things I share with them, I would be able to reach more people and really make a difference.

When I started to gather my thoughts on the best way to share my insights, it seemed to come in three distinct categories, each a little different yet blended with the common theme of the magic of energy. I've prepared this book in three sections, of which one, none, or all may resonate with you. All I ask is that you read it with an open heart and open mind, and in the end, if one single idea or sentence helps you feel a little lighter or view yourself or other people a little more favorably, then my goal will have been met.

The first section is about the magic of energy and

how becoming aware of it can alter your everyday life and help you see others and the world with new eyes. It will help you realize that you control your energy, the way you feel, and ultimately, your effect on others. Once you are aware of and can clear your own energy, you will feel like a new person.

The second section is about working with energy. Once your energy is clear, you'll be able to start "reading" other people's energy and have a positive, sometimes life-changing, effect on them. It discusses how to tune in to others' energy, both people and animals, and how to help them either verbally or with hands-on energy work. I share my experiences learning about hands-on energy specifically from horses, but these learnings can be applied to any person or animal. It also discusses the valuable lessons I've learned from hands-on work that are outside the teachings in formal energy disciplines.

If this section resonates with you, I can't stress enough the necessity to incorporate the information from Section 1. You must be aware of and clear your own energy before working on others. Whether you do or do not want to actively interact and help others, some of the lessons in this brief section may still resonate and apply to your everyday life and your interactions with others.

The final section talks about how you can take energy work to a higher level. I share my journey of discovering who I am, what this journey is all about, and what my so-called purpose is. My journey involved horses, human mentors, and lots and lots of reading, seminars, and training with amazing people who have even more amazing gifts to share. I had so many questions along the way, and now, when I speak to various people who are on different parts of their own journey, they seem to have the same questions. I'm not in any way saying I have the answers, but I have found that by sharing some of the things I've experienced and learned, I've been able to help others get closer to realizing their own purpose on this journey.

To start this journey, let's first talk about what energy is.

SECTION 1

What Is Energy and How Does It Affect Me?

Chapter 1: What's Your Energy?

Energy: what a simple word for an all-encompassing concept.

Everyone and everything is made up of energy, and everyone and everything both receive and put out energy. Yet most of us are completely unaware of the energy we are putting out (through everything we think, say, and do) and the effect our energy has on everyone around us and the universe as a whole.

How can you become aware of what your energy consists of? How can you change or modify it if needed, and why is that important? To start with, let me point out that the head and the heart are generally thought of as the two main portals of the body that receive information (hence the references to thinking with your head or feeling with your heart).

But the actual storage of your so-called energy resides in your gut. This is why the saying "a gut feeling" is commonly associated with your intuition. Your gut, or stomach area, houses the various emotions you feel. When something happens that annoys or angers you, or you feel frustrated, slighted, or insulted, you get a comparable feeling in your gut. It tenses up and you may feel responses in other parts of your body, like your heart racing or your jaw clenching.

While it's normal for us to have emotional reactions to the people and circumstances surrounding us in every-day life, problems arise when we don't actually process and release those energies. When we hold on to them, not only do they have the potential to negatively affect our physical health, but they also make us feel negative, which in turn makes us cranky, irritable, and generally unhappy.

An interesting example is when I was driving to an event, and my friend was following in the car behind me. There was a lot of traffic, and another driver swerved out to jump into a turn lane and then back into traffic and cut me off. I was able to react quickly, thank goodness, and avoided an accident. I noticed him do it a few more times, much to the irritation of all the other drivers.

Later, when we arrived at the event, my friend was fuming and talking about "that crazy idiot." He wanted to know why I didn't react and yell or honk. I honestly had to stop, think, and ask, "What are you talking about?" Here he was, all full of stress and ranting about the incident with the other driver, while I had already processed and released it. As it was no longer on my mind, I was free and feeling good, but he was stressed, agitated, and in a foul mood.

Why let someone have that kind of power over you? Isn't it better to process and release? The driver was no longer there and, in all likelihood, didn't even know my friend was upset. So what purpose was it serving? Process it and let it go!

Hiding Our Emotions

I find it interesting that humans are the only species that lies and hides their emotions. With animals, what you see is what you get. If a horse encounters a wolf in the wild, it instantly knows the wolf's intent by the energy the wolf is putting out. Either it's hungry and looking to attack, or it's just eaten and has no intention of attacking. It doesn't "pretend" to not be a threat until it gets close and can then attack. The energy it puts out is open and honest, and the horse can rely on that and either run for safety or stay and graze accordingly.

But as humans, we try to deceive ourselves and those around us. Although we're feeling all those negative emotions that have been bottled up inside us, we put on a happy face. When people ask how we are, we say, "Great!" We may even believe it ourselves. However, our energy never lies, and those negative feelings are right below the surface, ready to boil up and explode when the next negative event occurs. And then maybe we blow up at the poor, unsuspecting people around us for something tiny. (We've all been on both the giving and receiving end of that.)

Having become masters of deception regarding our emotions, we can fool many people—and even ourselves—but intuitive people and animals will see through it every time. That's because animals don't listen to your words; they simply read your energy. So much so, in fact, that it confuses and scares them when a person's words or portrayal directly conflict with the energy they are putting out. Animals are the litmus test in helping you identify your true feelings and the energy you are putting out.

An example of this is a situation that occurred with my horse Midnight, who is an amazing teacher and guide and whom I will reference often in my stories and examples. Once, when I was going out of town, a friend asked if it was okay to give Midnight treats while I was gone. Of course I said yes, as Midnight loved to devour them. One day soon after I returned, I was working with him when the friend approached, so I didn't really turn to her to pick up her energy. After a few minutes, I turned to talk to her about how Midnight had done while I was gone, and she said that she was baffled because not only did he not take any treats from her while I was away, but he also wouldn't even let her touch him. I looked over and, to my surprise, Midnight had backed himself into a corner, as far away from her as he could get.

This was baffling. Midnight is a very social horse who loves people, attention, and treats. So I turned to look at her, immediately assessed her energy, and asked, "What's wrong?" With a big smile on her face, she insisted nothing was wrong and everything was great. I looked her in the eye and said, "Then why is there smoke coming out your ears?" (Which is how I would describe her energy at that moment.)

She suddenly started to cry and told me that her husband had had a heart attack, lost his job, and that they would have to move and sell her beloved horse. Any one of those events would have been difficult to deal with, but all of them at once would be overwhelming. As we started to chat about it, Midnight came up behind her and, while she was crying, gently put his head over her shoulder in comfort. Her surprise was genuine, and she was baffled.

I explained to her that her words and actions had been in direct contrast to what she was feeling inside. Although she had been talking to Midnight and others with the facade that everything was fine, her energy was screaming that everything was wrong. As I mentioned, only humans display this disparity, and so Midnight, without being able to determine clear intent, rightfully backed away to protect himself. Then, once she admitted what the circumstances were and started crying, her emotions and energy fell in line with what her words and actions were saying and doing. Now that her intentions were clear and the conflict removed, Midnight could trust what she was putting out and felt safe to approach and console her.

Another example is when they say a horse can "sense" your fear. What is actually happening is that, although you pretend to be confident and calm through your voice and movement, the horse is reading your energy, which is screaming "I'm scared," and the horse reacts accordingly.

In hindsight, I now know why I would get uncomfortable in groups of people who knew each other. It wasn't until I learned more about energy and the facade people hide behind that I realized that, like Midnight, when I felt the direct contrast between what someone was saying and the energy they were putting out, it threw me off and caused me to back away. Don't judge yourself if you've been guilty of this. We all do it. When you're talking one-on-one with someone, they can be very present and honest, but as soon as a third person joins the conversation, their energy changes. The person raises their energy to what I call the "public persona," where they put on a happy face and hide what they're truly feeling.

Your Energy Always Tells the Truth

The first lesson to learn is that, regardless of the front you put on, the energy you put out to those around you is always the actual energy you feel inside. If you're angry but say you're fine, you're actually putting out negative energy to those around you, and that negative energy has a ripple effect.

As I mentioned in the introduction, ever since I was a child, I was easily able to pick up on and read other people's real energy. When a friend, or even a stranger, would start talking about a decision they made or something they were going to do, as opposed to simply listening to what they were saying, I was feeling what their energy was screaming. They might be verbally stating that they were happy or excited about a decision, but their energy was screaming it wasn't right for them or they weren't happy with the decision. Then, while we were talking, I would be able to easily guide them to what they already knew internally was best for them but had not been able to mentally acknowledge. They would leave feeling so relieved and happy, thanking me for what they thought was wise advice but in reality was actually me simply interpreting their own energy to them.

At the time, I wasn't aware of what I was doing and thought everyone could see, sense, and feel the same energy in others that I could. I was baffled as to why they couldn't see their situation clearly by themselves. It wasn't until I started my journey of actively exploring energy, with the help of many wise and amazing teachers, both human and animal, that I learned what was actually occurring.

However, although I could easily see, sense, and feel others' true energy in the beginning of my journey, I hadn't yet realized that, like everyone else, I was also internally holding all the various emotions I encountered in everyday life. Those unreleased emotions were affecting not only my health but also the way I felt and the energy I was putting out. As I started to actively explore and learn about energy, I was able to realize the power of identifying, owning, and releasing the various emotions I experienced. I found that releasing energy not only made me feel so free and happy, but it also actually changed the way I viewed other people. Now, instead of judging or trying to change or fix people, I see them clearly for who they are, in their own unique and beautiful way.

Instead of trying to hide how you really feel, let's work on actually changing how you feel so that the energy you put out is pure, honest, and positive. Why? Because the energy you put out to the universe has a ripple effect and ends up coming back to you tenfold. Positive energy attracts more positive energy, and negative energy attracts negative energy. When we talk about karma, it doesn't mean revenge or justice; it simply means we envelop and receive the energy that we ourselves put out.

You don't have to change how you handle your energy overnight. To start, simply be open to coming to terms with what you're truly feeling and ask yourself how you can honestly and openly change those feelings to the positive.

You'll be amazed not only by how wonderful you feel but also by how differently you view the world and other people. The new you will truly feel and put out so much beautiful, positive energy that it will become contagious to other people who cross your path. Suddenly, you'll notice positive things occurring all around you.

Are you ready?

———————

Chapter 2: Changing Your Energy

I find it interesting that although we experience positive and negative emotions every day, we tend to hold on to the negative energy. And unfortunately, we tend to quickly pass over the positive energies. As a result, the negative ones build and build inside us until they overwhelm us, and there's no room for the positive ones.

The first step on the path to change your energy is to focus on what generates negative emotions.

Ego

Ego shouldn't be confused with self-esteem, pride, or self-love, as you need to like, love, and feel happy about yourself in order to see the good in others.

As humans, we tend to be ego-oriented and view the world and actions of others from the perspective of how they affect us. We judge people for how we think they should feel, act, and be as opposed to simply seeing them as they are.

For example, think about the last time you tried to drive through a crowded parking lot. As people crossed your path, moseying to and from their cars, you probably thought, "Walk faster already!" But later, when you finished your shopping and walked back to your own car, you saw cars pushing through and thought, "The pedestrian has the right of way. Slow down!" We tend to view and judge others' behaviors by how they affect us *in that moment.*

We also tend to judge others based on the way we do things. For example, if you drive slowly, you think those fast drivers are maniacs. If you're a fast driver, you think other drivers are slowpokes always in the way. Or consider the harsh judgment from the person who believes you must be orderly and wait your turn in line toward the person who pushes ahead and forces their way in.

But just because others do things differently than you doesn't mean you should judge them. It will only get you upset and out of sorts. It's not worth it. After all, your judgment will make no difference to them, and the reality is your way is not the only and absolute way. Start broadening your outlook!

In this next example, I've made up numbers because the numbers themselves aren't important. The concept I want to convey is that humans tend to see things in a limited manner.

Envision a twenty-foot-diameter circle surrounding you. You're standing in the middle, and everything from the perimeter of the circle is pointing in toward you. You have limited vision and view everyone and everything only from the viewpoint of how they affect you.

Horses, on the other hand, are prey animals, which means they need to always be aware of any threats in their environment. Their circle of awareness is much larger, easily spanning one hundred feet in diameter. And instead of everything from the perimeter pointing toward them, all their focus is pointing out. This means that instead of focusing on themselves, they are always aware of what is going on around them. They see things and people as they are without judgment.

Try expanding your circle and switching your arrows outward instead of inward. You'll be amazed at how differently you see things!

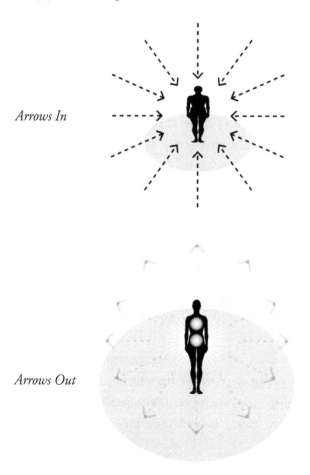

Arrows In

Arrows Out

Another issue that comes up when we are ego-focused is the idea of right and wrong. How do you feel when you're wrong about something that you really thought was right? Do you feel hurt, angry, or defensive? Does your ego take a hit? Be honest with yourself, because changing how you feel about being wrong can change your whole outlook on life and allow you to take more chances. So many times in the past I was so adamant that I was right about something that when I finally realized I was actually wrong, it blew my mind.

Back then, any time I was wrong, my ego really took a hit. Suddenly I wasn't as smart or experienced as I thought I was. But as I've grown energetically, I'm now able to release any negative energy associated with being wrong and instead embrace it as a learning experience. Now I actually love being wrong because it means I've just learned something new, which is great! I don't measure my progress by how often I'm right but how often I'm wrong because that means I'm learning—and when you stop learning, you stop living.

I love the meaningful saying, "You can disappoint people and still be good enough. You can fail and still be smart, capable, and talented. You can let people down and still be worthy of love and admiration." Stop being your own worst critic. Put yourself out there and take chances.

I encourage you to make learning one new thing every day a habit. And when you're wrong about something, you can say, "Hey, I learned something new and met my quota today!"

The Amazing Effect of Changing Your Energy

One of my favorite sayings is, "Everyone wants to change the world, but no one wants to change themselves." Changing means you're learning and growing.

In this next section, I am going to challenge you to be open to making small changes to yourself. Even if you read this and think, "That doesn't apply to me," give it a chance. Try the suggestions once or twice and be open to what happens. You may be totally amazed by the outcome. "Open heart, open mind" is the key to personal growth. And keep in mind that when I use the word *change*, I don't mean changing *who you are*. You are beautiful and amazing just as you are. I mean changing the way you *feel* and the way you *see* others in order to become a better you.

One of my favorite examples of this happened when I was volunteering for a program that pairs veterans with horses, who are natural healers and often used therapeutically to help people. I was working with one man who was paired with a very easygoing horse, and the two really bonded as he softly brushed the horse and spoke with him. It was amazing to see his transformation, as he had arrived tense and guarded, but the horse was able to break through his barrier, and the man ended up hugging the horse, smiling and saying he had a new best friend.

Then, we moved to another horse, and as he approached the horse, the horse got rigid and pinned his ears back, which is a sign of aggression. The man immediately recoiled, tensed up, and backed away. He stated that he didn't like this horse and didn't want to work with him.

I told him I understood his concern, and that he was definitely picking up the right energy from the horse. Then I mentioned that the horse seemed to be defensive, thus the resulting negative energy. He agreed wholeheartedly. So I asked him, "What can you do to make him feel a little less defensive?" He thought about it for a few minutes and then slowly started to softly groom the horse and talk to him quietly. Immediately, the horse's demeanor changed; he relaxed and started nuzzling his newfound friend. By the time they were done, the man stated that now this was his new best friend, and he wanted to work with this horse in all the following sessions. I agreed and then asked him what he did to change the horse's demeanor so drastically and quickly. He thought about it and said, "I changed *my* energy."

He was absolutely right, and therein lies the power! By simply choosing to change your own energy, you can positively affect the energy of everyone around you.

When you come across a negative or angry person, instead of becoming negative, which in turn just escalates the situation, try to see what the person is feeling that is making them act that way. Then, see if there's a way you can help them feel differently. Instead of both of you feeling negative and looking for a fight, you can actually help that person feel better. There's an important caveat however: Do not try to change others. Simply let your energy change the way they feel for the better.

In the example above, we may never know who started the negative energy. Was the horse reacting to the negative energy the man was carrying, or was the horse having a bad day and putting out its own negative energy? The bottom line is, it doesn't matter. Simply by changing his energy, the veteran was able to change the situation from a negative experience to a positive one, resulting in both of them feeling happy and light.

Remember, in every situation you encounter, you control how you approach it: positively or negatively. Will you escalate a simmering negative interaction or defuse it by softening your view of the person and not judging, hopefully leaving that person feeling a little bit better for having crossed your path that day? The choice is yours.

It's Not About You! (Back to That Ego Again)

One of the greatest lessons I've learned on this journey is that the majority of what people think, say, and do has absolutely nothing to do with me. Instead, it's a reflection of them and what they're feeling or going through. So when you get angry at the person who cut you off in the grocery store with their cart, realize that, in all likelihood, they probably didn't even notice you. If you're in a social setting and someone makes a snide remark you are certain was directed at you, in all likelihood, it reflected something they were dealing with and had nothing to do with you. Stop making things about yourself.

Instead of judging, try to view others' behavior as a reflection of how they feel about themselves. Happy people like themselves and see the good in others, and unhappy people tend to see and act negatively.

Think about it. We've all been the person, or around a

person, who is newly in love. It's a wonderful feeling, and the person is over-the-moon happy, seeing the good and the beauty in everything and everyone. They dance around and want everyone to be as happy as they are. Their energy is contagious.

The same goes for the opposite. When someone is insecure, nasty, impatient, and intolerant, it's because they're miserable. Misery loves company, so miserable people put out miserable energy, wanting everyone around them to feel the same. If everyone is miserable, they can feel "normal" and convince themselves that they're not the issue. But just like the encounter with the man and the horse, you have the power to change every situation to a positive encounter.

Judgment Equals Negative Emotion

We talked about the feeling in your gut when you have an emotional response. It's important to notice how different emotions generate different feelings in your gut. When something happens that pleases us, we get a soft, light, good feeling in our gut. But when something happens that displeases us, whether intentional or from our judgment of another, we get a tight, clenched feeling in our gut.

You may have had that tight, clenched feeling for so long that you don't even realize it's there. In fact, it's so built up that you don't have room for the soft, light, good feelings.

On your journey to identifying and releasing stored emotions, you may find your mind trying to trick you. It will try to fool you with words. You'll find yourself thinking or saying, "I'm not any better than anyone else, just different based on my experiences on this journey," and believing that you are releasing judgment. However, the one thing you can't fool yourself with is how you feel in your gut—that negative reaction inside you will out you every time.

An example of this occurred one day when I was doing energy work on various horses with an amazing veterinarian (one of my mentors). They all took the energy well until we started working on one particular horse. This horse was unhappy and defensive, and no matter what we did, he was difficult to work with. I thought to myself that it wasn't his fault he was acting up; it was the way his person handled him that was causing him to be so defensive.

Because I had been working for some time on releasing negative energies within myself, I was pretty clear energetically, so it was easy for me to immediately identify when I was taking on a negative emotion. And I was definitely feeling negative emotions right then. I felt frustrated and angry that the poor horse was dealing with such negative interactions with its person, and I felt angry that the entire situation could have been avoided through better treatment.

That evening, I tried to release the negative feelings I had brought upon myself, with no luck. The next morning as I was riding my bike, which is my form of meditation, I again tried to clear the emotions, and again was unsuccessful. Finally, I opened myself up to all the possible reasons this negativity was stuck, and immediately, I received the thought, "It's your ego." I immediately denied it, saying, "I don't think I'm better than she is," (referring to that horse's person). The response was quick: "But you think your way is better than hers." I immediately thought, "Well yeah, because my way *is* better than hers!"

Finally, it clicked. By thinking my way was better, I was actually judging her by my standards, and thus thinking I was better than her.

Once I identified, admitted, and owned the negative feeling, I was able to process and release it. With a softer eye, I could now see that her actions were based on what she had been taught and experienced, and she simply didn't know any other way. Now that I saw her differently, the next time I ran into her at the barn, I had no feelings of frustration or anger.

The beauty of this example is that once I stopped judging and criticizing her, I noticed her starting to mimic the way I interacted with my horse. A short time later, I was thrilled to see a positive change in her horse. Notice that she didn't change her behavior because of anything I said, rather, when I stopped judging her and sending out negative energy, she became more open and learned by observing.

Exercise One: Identifying Emotion Triggers

Think about someone in your life, whether a family member or acquaintance, who seems to push your buttons every time you see them. Take a moment to objectively identify what about that person triggers your negative response(s).

Once you've identified your trigger, identify what is *causing* the trigger. I've found it's generally one of two things: "you spot it, you got it" or judgment.

"You spot it, you got it" is when you find—if you're honest with yourself—the trait they're displaying is one you don't like in yourself. It takes a lot of humility to admit it's a trait you mirror, but if you can be open to the realization, you can start the process of making a change and becoming a better, happier person.

On the other hand, if you can honestly say it's not a trait you have, then you have judged how they should act and be by your standards. Who are you to judge?

After you've identified the trait that annoys you in that person, take a moment to think about what that indicates about them and really see them for the vulnerable, hurt being they are. Instead of seeing the bully who always has to be the center of attention, see the wounded soul that is covering up their insecurity and lack of self-worth. If they are constantly criticizing you, realize that they're criticizing you because they aren't happy with themselves.

Once you realize it isn't about you and stop making judgments, you will truly see that person in a different, softer way and find yourself being much more tolerant. Instead of having them negatively affect you, you soften and send out healing, positive energy as opposed to hard, critical energy.

The next time you see this person, try to see why they are acting like they are, and instead of judging them for it, ask yourself how you could maybe make them feel a little better about themselves. Maybe it's simply listening to them in a nonjudgmental way or offering them a smile and putting out your good energy. Sometimes just letting someone know you really see them and are listening can have an amazing healing effect.

Make it a habit to not respond with negative energy whenever you encounter someone with negative energy. Soften your eyes, see the reason for their energy, diffuse the situation, and send them positive energy. Don't try to change their energy; let your positive energy do the work.

Exercise Two: Stop Contagious Negativity in Its Tracks

Negative energy is contagious! I have another challenge for you. The next time you're with a group of people and they begin talking negatively about a person you all know, don't jump on board (not even if they are right about the negative aspects or traits). Instead of adding fuel to the fire, take a moment to step back, think of a single positive thing you can say about that person, and point out that positive aspect to the group.

If you can't think of one nice thing to say about someone, that's a sure sign that you're looking at them through judgment-colored lenses! Take off those lenses and really see the person as the beautiful soul they are, and I guarantee you'll find something good about them.

It's important to remember that you're not disagreeing or challenging those who are speaking negatively. By shifting the focus to a positive trait, you shift the energy in the group and maybe even soften the way they view others.

People learn by example. Don't be the one who joins in and compounds the negative; be the one who softens and helps others soften too. Ultimately, you are the winner, as you will leave feeling light and happy as opposed to righteous and judgmental. Be sure to notice and compliment people when you see them doing something kind, as opposed to criticizing them when they are critical or negative. Criticism puts up walls; compliments open doors.

Avoid Reinforcing Negativity through Complaining

Complaining is a waste of time. It only reinforces the negative emotions within you and sends out negative energy to those around you. In the next chapter, you'll learn how to clear your energy, letting you release any negative energy as quickly as you encounter it so you'll have no need to complain. However, until you have mastered that lesson, it's okay to vent *once in a while* to help you release negative energy.

What's the difference between complaining and venting? When you complain, you're continuously sending out negative energy while whining that you're unhappy because something isn't the way you think or want it to be, and you're not offering any potential solutions. Venting is a one-time release of the negative emotion, and you're either accepting the situation as it is (you simply need to vocalize it once to release it) or you're actively looking for potential solutions to the situation.

When you find yourself complaining, take a moment

to determine the source. Did it arise from something negatively affecting you or because you judged someone else? If it's judgment, let it go. If it is something that negatively affects you, determine if there's a viable solution. In those (hopefully few) situations where there are no viable solutions, you need to either accept it as is or walk away. Either way, stop complaining, because all the complaining in the world isn't going to change it. Let it go!

To Recap

Remember, no one can make you feel a certain way. Any negative feeling you experience comes directly from how you choose to interpret someone else's actions. If you see it as being about you and judge them, you will feel a negative emotion. If you choose to remember that their words and actions reflect how they feel about themselves, resist judgment and become more understanding; not only do you not get that awful negative feeling, but you'll actually feel light and happy. Even better, you will most likely pass that positive energy on to them and help them heal without even trying.

The key is to be aware and honest with yourself about what you're truly feeling. Change your perspective so that the arrows are pointed out instead of in, and start seeing the world and the people in it in a softer, more beautiful way.

Chapter 3: Releasing Stored Negative Energy

Now that you know how to stop taking on new negative emotions, you can start identifying the emotions you are currently holding—ones you've likely been holding on to for quite some time. It's important you learn to identify and release this old negative energy so the base state of your gut is clear. That way, when you receive a new negative emotion, you can quickly and easily feel and release it. I'll be honest with you: This is not an easy process. It requires you to be honest and open with yourself, and it will take both time and effort on your part.

Because you've been storing these negative energies for a long time, there will be layers of energy to clear. To start, without thinking and being completely honest, quickly respond to the following question: What is the strongest feeling in your gut right now? Is your gut free and light, or is there a tight or uncomfortable feeling in it? You'll most likely respond with the latter. That's okay.

The next step is to try to identify that feeling. Is it anger, fear, frustration, hurt, tenseness, anxiety, or irritation?

Once you identify it, think about what caused it. If it came from a specific situation with another person, use what we've learned so far and try to see it from a different perspective, remembering that their actions reflect them, not you. If it's not from a specific situation, ask yourself if it's either a "you spot it, you got it" or a judgment situation.

When it comes to releasing stored energy, you first have to be honest about what you're feeling and why. Then you have to own it. That means you accept the fact that "they" didn't make you feel a certain way. Once you identify and own it, you can then release it simply by letting go of the judgment. It's natural and okay to judge; the danger comes when you don't process it and let it go.

Positive Energy Providers: Motivators

Think of someone in your life who always leaves you feeling lighter, calmer, happier, and more confident after you see them. It could be a family member, friend, neighbor, acquaintance, coworker, or even a cashier or receptionist at a place you frequent.

Take a moment to assess them. They likely share two common traits: they like themselves, and they are not judging you. Take in how that feels. Now take a moment to think about how many people cross your path daily that you can honestly say would choose you as a person who makes them feel good. Be honest with yourself.

Do you leave people feeling better or worse about themselves after they see you? Did you offer unsolicited advice? Remember that unsolicited advice is no longer advice—it's criticism. Even if you have good intentions because you think you can help them, be open-minded and realize you may not be right. And even if you are, they may not be ready.

Whether or not your observation is accurate, you are not compelled to say it. Realize that the person may have been having a good day, feeling happy and good about themselves, and out of the blue, you're "giving them advice" on how they need to change themselves or the way they are living. Now, not only are they unlikely to embrace your intentions, but they will likely resist it and walk away feeling deflated. They thought they were having a good day, and now they've been told they need to fix themselves.

Remember, people learn by example and by receiving positive energy and feedback, not by being criticized. Being criticized not only causes a person to put up walls in defense but also leaves them feeling depleted.

Negative Energy Providers: Vampires

Now let's look at the other side: Are there people in your life you dread seeing? Every time you see them, they seem to drain your energy and leave you feeling exhausted and depressed. People with this type of energy are often referred to as vampires, as they seem to suck the life right out of you.

Here's a reality check that you're not going to like—it's not them, it's you.

What do I mean by that? Well, good energy is limitless. If your gut is clear of all those negative emotions and judgments, and you're feeling good, you actually draw in good energy from above, and it flows down through your head to your heart and then into your gut. You, in turn, beam that energy out to everyone around you. As long as your energy is clear, there is no limit to your ability to absorb that amazing energy, and the more you spread it to others, the more you can take in.

But if your gut is filled with negative emotion, the flow stops there as it gets blocked. When there's a blockage and the energy can't flow out and be shared, you can no longer draw more positive energy into yourself, because there is nowhere for it to go.

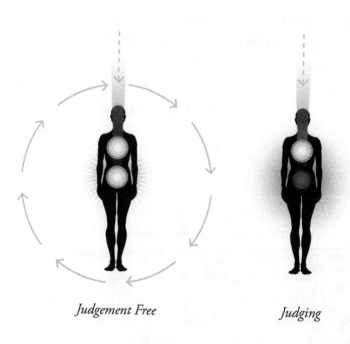

Judgement Free   *Judging*

What does this have to do with vampires? When you see the person you designate as the vampire, and they start to complain (or do whatever action you say drains you), you judge that person and immediately stop the energy flow. So when you leave, you feel drained, annoyed, and frustrated because *you* blocked the flow, and there is no more good energy coming into you. Your energy is stagnant.

But the reality is they didn't "take" or "drain" your energy. Instead, you blocked the flow of energy into your gut yourself. Only you can determine when and how your energy is blocked, and the less judgmental you are, the lighter you'll feel your energy becoming.

But remember, what people think, say, and do is a reflection of them, and the hardest ones to love are the ones that need it the most. Stop for a moment, look for why that so-called vampire is behaving that way, and try to see them for the troubled soul they are. Instead of judging them, continue to put out your good energy to them. By not judging, you keep that negative emotion from your belly, and the energy flow can continue.

As long as you keep putting out the good energy to them, you can take on more good energy and not end up feeling drained and empty. There is no limit to how much good energy you can put out to others.

It's critical that you acknowledge others' energy without taking it on. Don't tell them why they shouldn't feel a certain way, because whether they should or shouldn't is irrelevant. The bottom line is they *do* feel that way. Acknowledge it without taking it on, and then send out your positive, unjudging energy, and you'll be amazed by the results. By looking at the person with soft eyes and trying to understand how they feel—without trying to change or fix them—you are much more likely to have a positive effect on them and maybe even help them find their way.

I challenge you to do two things. First, at the end of the day, take an honest assessment of the people you interacted with, even if only for a moment. How many of those people walked away feeling happier than before they saw you? And how many, if you're honest with yourself, likely walked off feeling deflated, defensive, misunderstood, criticized, angry, frustrated, or ignored? Your goal is to increase the number of people in the first category by one each day until it becomes a habit and you do it without thinking about it.

Once you've mastered that, the second challenge is to think about any so-called vampires that you encountered. Were you able to see them with soft eyes, not judge, and leave them feeling better? Or did you judge, stop the energy flow, and leave both of you feeling worse? This takes time to master, and you need to be honest with yourself along the way. Being aware is the first step. After the first time you're successful—when you actually see that vampire differently and both of you leave the interaction feeling good—you'll be astonished at the difference and want to incorporate it in to your daily life. Eventually, if you embrace this and make it a daily habit, you'll find that you don't have any more "vampires" in your life.

Clearing Your Own Energy

In Section 2, we'll talk about how to become aware of and read other people's energy. However, it's extremely important that you don't start this practice until you have successfully cleared your own energy. So let's explore a few ways to do just that.

First, do a physical energy check on yourself. Start with your face: Is there a smile or a frown? Is your jaw clenched or soft? Then move on to the rest of your body. Are you standing slumped, with the top of your body collapsing down onto your belly? Are you looking down and away? Your body reflects your energy and vice versa, so you want your body open and free.

Imagine a string coming down from the sky; let it attach to your head. Now imagine that string pulling the top of your head up, up, up, which in turn lifts up your shoulders and ribs. It then lightens your chest and stomach and allows your hips and feet to fall freely to the ground. Be sure your chin is up and you're not only looking forward, but you're also "seeing" what's in front of and around you. Be present in the moment! Feel how good it feels to be open, free, and light, moving forward with positive energy and a smile on your face. Do this exercise multiple times a day, every day, until you find yourself doing it without even thinking.

It's also critical for you to take time for yourself to clear your own energy, using whatever method works for you. Some people enjoy meditation, but that's not the only way. Some will sit outside, quietly enjoying nature. Others find they calm and clear themselves in everyday actions, such as taking a shower, riding the lawn mower, or washing dishes. For me, it's riding my bicycle out in the open, noticing and embracing everything around me; or when I'm alone with my horses, peacefully walking with them as they graze. You don't have to formally meditate—just find what works for you and make time to do it as often as you can.

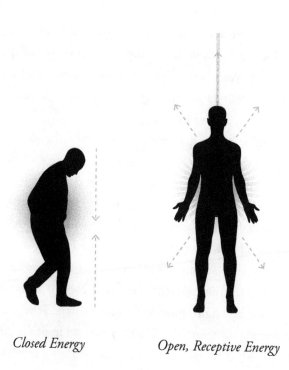

Closed Energy   *Open, Receptive Energy*

To help you really release anything you're holding on to, try this breathing exercise. Take a deep breath in while you count to four. Then exhale deeply, counting to five. *The exhale is extremely important as it releases any negative energy.* (Many people will inhale deeply but follow it with a shallow exhale and never really release the stagnant energy.) After an inhale for four and an exhale for five, increase the count by one for both (inhale for five, exhale for six; inhale for six, exhale for seven; etc.). Keep going until you feel free and released. This is another exercise to do multiple times a day, every day, but especially when you want to clear any negative energy that you're carrying— both in your gut and in your head.

Speaking of the necessity of clearing your energy, I want to share with you a lesson I learned from a very wise little girl. Any parent or person who has worked with children knows that you have to be careful what "promises" you make to a small child, as they will remember them and call you out if you don't deliver. This little girl was telling me about something her mother promised her they would do that day, but the mother had forgotten. She calmly explained to me that children remember everything because they don't have so much "stuff" in their heads to get in the way. Adults have too much "stuff." The truth of that statement really resonated with me. It's a reminder that we all need to clear the compilation of useless "stuff" in our heads that has accumulated over the years so we can feel clearer and more open.

As you practice clearing your own energy, here are a few things to keep in mind.

Don't surround yourself only with people who think the same as you do. Make sure you include people who challenge you to grow and think outside the box. Remember, when two people agree on everything, it means only one person is doing the thinking.

Don't just tolerate difference; seek it out and embrace it. If we were all the same, how boring would that be? Be open to alternative ideas, experiences, and practices that are new to you. Learn, experience, grow, and share.

Don't internalize hurt. If someone hurts you, realize that what they said or did was about them, not you. Then soften, own, and release. (I can't say this enough!)

Forgiveness is for you, not for them. When you hold resentment or anger toward someone, you're only hurting yourself, both emotionally and physically. You're not hurting them; most likely, they don't even know you're angry. Forgiving someone doesn't mean you excuse what they did or said. It means you are letting go of the negative emotion that resulted. Once you release it, you will feel better, lighter, and more likely to be able to see the person in a softer way. This doesn't mean you put yourself back in a position where they can hurt you again. Instead, now that you're stronger, you'll realize their actions or words are about them, not you, and therefore, you'll be less likely to judge them. As a result, their ability to hurt you is diffused. Forgiveness always feels much better than holding on to pain.

Stop holding grudges. Grudges are self-righteous and the biggest waste of energy. Remember, you feel a grudge because you judged someone, and right or wrong, the reality is that they don't even realize you're holding a grudge. Yet every time you think of or see them, you get that grudge feeling in the pit of your stomach, and it makes you feel negative. Let it go and see how much better that feels.

Don't waste time. Is there someone you love that you're holding at arm's length because something they said or did offended or annoyed you? If so, stop making it about you, let go of grudges, and embrace them now while you can. You will never get this missed time with them back again!

Be open to the prospect that someone has grown and changed. We tend to judge people based on what we perceive as their negative traits, and we hold on to that judgment forever. Often, even when the person has been able to improve themselves—maybe even eliminate those so-called negative traits completely—we continue to see them through the same old lenses. That's why you often hear people say they can't go back home after moving away and growing because the people there still see them as who they were all those years ago. Throw out those judgmental lenses, and fairly and clearly see each person for who they are right now, in the moment, not with preconceived notions of who they used to be. You may be surprised.

Do an honest self-check. When you first see someone, be it a stranger or someone you know, is the first thing you notice something positive about them or something negative? The first thing you notice tends to be a reflection of the energy you are putting out. If you're putting out negative energy, you'll likely notice negative things in others. But if you're putting out positive energy, you'll tend to see the best in others. Even more interesting, you will get what you're looking for. If you expect to see the negative, you will. So why not expect the positive and relish in what you find? It's your choice.

Do something kind, without expecting anything in return, not even a thank you. The beautiful, light feeling you get from putting positive energy out will be your reward. Even more important, don't just "do" something kind, "be" kind.

At the end of each day, take a moment to reflect on how you spent or shared your energy. Are you pleased with your interactions and feeling light and happy? Or were you short with someone who could have used just two minutes of your time, but you were too busy to be bothered? Were your arrows pointed out, or were you the center of your focus? Be honest with yourself, and then make a plan on how you can do better tomorrow. It doesn't have to be something grand as it's the small things that make a difference.

Before I started my journey of actively learning about energy, even with my self-perceived harsh and judgmental ways, people still seemed drawn to me and my energy. It's like my soft soul was always there, but it was encased in a hard shell of judgment and righteousness. Thank goodness my real energy shone through so I could still help people without realizing it until I learned through my journey how to shed that shell. You, too, can shed your hard shell and help others.

To Recap

Remember, it's easier to blame others for the way you feel instead of taking ownership of it and changing it, but it is definitely worth the effort. I can say this because all the negative attributes and challenging things I reference in this chapter I've been guilty of myself. But through amazing mentors, both human and horses, I was able to change the way I viewed people and their actions, and I came out on the other side stronger and feeling the power of absolute love and acceptance. You can too.

SECTION 2

Working with Energy

Chapter 4: Tune In to Energy

You probably already "sense" energy. How many times have you felt a car was coming into your lane before it happened or felt the eyes of someone across the room boring into you, and when you look up, you immediately make eye contact? In both instances, you were subliminally sensing energy.

However, to intentionally sense someone else's energy clearly, you need to be clear and quiet yourself. The quieter and clearer your energy is, the more you're able to pick up on the energy around you. When it's noisy in your head, you won't be able to hear anything else. Think of the adage, "When you speak, it's silent. When you're silent, it speaks." This applies both to the energy around you and receiving energy or information from your intuition.

You can receive information from your intuition even if you haven't practiced reading or hearing energy yet, as long as you are quiet and listen. For example, many years ago, I was on a ski trip. I had been taught that to stay safe on more difficult runs, you should never take them alone, especially when they are above the area that the ski patrol monitors. While on this trip, my travel companions, who were not advanced skiers, wanted a break in the lodge, so I joined two other experienced skiers, and together, we enjoyed some of the tougher runs and terrain. As the day came to a close, a storm started rolling in. It was time to head back, but because we were from different lodges, we needed to take different trails, so we decided to split ways. Since I was alone, I stuck to one of the easy runs down.

As fate would have it, the storm accelerated quickly and brought with it a fog that greatly reduced visibility. As I was making a turn, unable to see well, I veered off the trail and slid down the side of the mountain, where my ski came off and disappeared deep into multiple feet of snow. I searched frantically for the missing ski with no luck. Looking around, I realized I was alone, three thousand feet up a mountain in an area where no other skiers would pass me. No one knew where I was—and the worst of the storm was quickly approaching. I was terrified, so I did what any well-trained outdoor athlete is trained to do in times of adversity: I sat down and cried.

After a few minutes, I was emotionally exhausted, leaving my brain quiet and empty. I looked up to the dark sky and said, out loud, "Mom, I need your help!" My mother had passed some years prior, and although I always knew she was with me, until that moment, I never really understood what that meant. Suddenly, the calmest feeling came over me. I stood up, walked about twenty feet diagonally downhill, and stuck my ski pole in the snow. There, about two feet deep in the snow, was my missing ski!

I was overjoyed. I quickly put my ski back on and made it back to the lodge safely, having learned a life lesson: your guides are always there and willing to help, but if there's too much noise in your head, you won't be able to hear them. Once I stopped panicking, released all my thoughts, and simply asked for help, I was able to hear my guides.

Fast forward twenty years. I had been working with my mentors on clearing my energy and expanding my intuition and communication for years, so I was more well-versed in how to hear and receive information. I had recently flown out of state to visit my father in his retirement home.

I'm usually very aware of my surroundings, especially when traveling, and I ensure I know where my valuables are at all times. One day, as visiting hours were coming to a close, I suddenly realized that my purse was missing. Frantically, I retraced my steps, asking everyone if they had seen it, to no avail. I was certain, given the surroundings, that no one had taken it, but that left me at a loss as to where it could be. Since I was traveling and needed ID to fly home, I was in a panic. Then I remembered: you can't hear or feel guidance when your head is full of thoughts. So I walked outside the room, exhaled deeply, and cleared all my thoughts and energy. Once I was fully clear, I said, "Mom, please show me where my purse is." I immediately received the information. It was on the back of the wheelchair of a lady I had stopped to help. When I had reached down to help her, my purse must have slid off my shoulder and onto the handles of her wheelchair.

I was thrilled I knew where it was, but now I had to find the lady and her chair. Some employees helped me figure out who she was (although I was kindly told that my description of "a nice, elderly lady with white hair in a wheelchair" is not a helpful identifier in a retirement home), and one even went ahead to the dining hall where they knew she was eating. However, they quickly returned saying my purse wasn't there. But the message I had received was so clear, and I had learned to trust the messages I received, so I insisted I look myself.

Sure enough, there was my purse, which had slid down the handles into a little cubby hole out of sight. It was so hidden that it may never have been found otherwise. But because I cleared my head and energy and opened myself to receiving, I was able to hear the message from my mother and find my purse.

You may have noticed that clearing my energy is not something I did once and never had to do again. Clearing yourself is something you need to do on an ongoing basis, sometimes even multiple times a day, especially if you're going through a particularly difficult or stressful time or are surrounded by a lot of emotionally charged people.

Expanding Your Awareness to Tune In to Energy

Once you are able to keep yourself open and clear, you'll be amazed at what you pick up that was always right before your eyes but you couldn't see. Energy is so powerful that animals can fully communicate without words, with absolutely no misunderstandings or cultural language barriers. With practice, you can too!

I find it interesting that although humans consider ourselves to be the advanced species, we're the only species that cannot communicate effectively with each other. We have so many different languages that when we meet people from other cultures, we often can't talk to or understand each other. Even when we speak the same language, words always get in the way. One person says something, and the other person misinterprets what they mean. People rely on literal words as opposed to feeling the emotions behind them.

In contrast, animals converse freely with each other regardless of species or geographic origin. Horses, dogs, cats, wolves, bears, and all other animals not only freely and accurately communicate nonverbally, but they are also never confused about their intent.

My beloved horse Chapiro is trained on voice commands in addition to being a natural at reading energy, and he knows exactly what I want when I say commands like "stay," "no," "drop it," or "wait." This means I don't need to restrain or confine him when I'm working with him, grooming him, or preparing to ride him. He'll simply wait patiently for my next command—usually.

At a certain point in our routine, I go get a special treat in the next room. Every time I say, "Absolutely no peeking!" And every time, he peeks around the corner. Even though I'm saying the negative "no" word, he can read the tone of my voice and the energy I'm putting out and knows that it's okay. Yet every single person who has observed this part of our routine has tried to keep him from peeking so he doesn't get in trouble. Chapiro is feeling the energy, while the humans are listening to the words.

I challenge you to put words aside and practice feeling the energy and meaning behind them. You'll be amazed at what you can learn.

Be Open and Aware of Nonverbal Communication

I've always loved watching the body language and silent communication among horses and have spent many enjoyable hours doing so. But it took two of my horses to teach me how to learn to feel nonverbal communication myself.

Midnight and Dalton are best buddies, and I'd often take them on a walk together to let them graze and stretch their legs. I kept Dalton on a lead rope but left Midnight free to walk as he pleased.

Whenever Dalton would suddenly raise his head to move to a completely different area, I would stop him, saying, "No, we need to wait for Midnight." It took me a long time to realize it, but Dalton wasn't the one making the decision—Midnight was, and he was energetically telling Dalton where and when to move. Once I realized this, and after much practice, I was actually able to "hear" Midnight's direction and react a split second before Dalton!

To be able to hear the communication between the two horses felt amazing and powerful. I had to laugh because as we would roam about, me with the lead rope on Dalton and Midnight directing from behind, people would always ask, "How did you train Midnight to follow you?" Of course, he wasn't following; he was directing. They were simply unaware of the silent communication happening.

This often happens because people tend to judge, think, and react based on their preconceived perception of what they think is occurring rather than what's actually happening.

Letting Go of Preconceived Perceptions

An example of this preconceived perception occurred with my horse Annie, an amazing and intuitive mare. Typically, when you are hand walking a horse to graze, you use a lead rope connected to the horse on one end, while you hold the other. The "perception" is that this keeps the horse from wandering or running off. One day, I decided to reward Annie by taking off the lead rope so that she could walk and graze wherever she chose. But she immediately became unhappy. She moved right next to me and pestered me until I put the lead rope back on. Only then did she calm down and happily start walking again.

At first, I was perplexed. But then I realized that in Annie's perspective, the lead rope hadn't been restraining her—it was restraining *me*. When it was attached, I couldn't wander off to do something else or talk with someone. It kept me focused on and present with her. We had two contrasting perceptions of the same situation. So when you start working to read others' energy, remember to keep an open mind to a different way of thinking. You may have some pleasant surprises!

One Person's Strength Can Be Another Person's Fear

Perceptions around fear can be another cause of miscommunication. One day, I was spending time with Midnight, who was grazing in a field that was adjacent to a busy road with lots of traffic. Unexpectedly, a helicopter flew over us, scaring Midnight, who started to bolt. I told him, "It's just a helicopter. Get over it!" A little while later, a huge 18-wheeler sped by us, and we got hit with a sudden backdraft. Again, Midnight started to bolt, and again, I said, "It's just a semi. Get over it!"

Not long after, a bee started buzzing around me, and I started doing the universal bee dance, frantically trying to get it away from me. Midnight came over, whapped the bee with his tail, and looked at me, very clearly saying, "It's a bee. Get over it!" I had to laugh, and I told him, "Point taken."

Remember that simply because something is irrelevant or simple to you doesn't mean it can't be a major issue or fear for someone else. Keep an open mind and broaden your perspective.

Diffuse Energy Like Horses

Over the years, I've found that horses are true masters of energy. I've been lucky enough to learn from Midnight and Annie how to diffuse negative energy by releasing positive, calming energy.

Annie is incredibly talented at diffusing the negative energy of anyone who visits her. I had a friend come out to the barn to visit once, and her energy was all over the place: agitated, over the top, and frenetic. As soon as I felt it, I handed her the lead rope to Annie and told her to go for a walk. An hour later, they emerged from the woods, and my friend was smiling, singing, and carefree. All her frenetic energy had dissipated. Annie had brought her into the present moment, helping her release her agitated energy and truly feel what it means to be happy.

Annie did this with everyone who came to visit. She would help them release all the negative emotions they were carrying and truly be present in the moment and happy. She absolutely would not put up with anyone who was not really present because they were absorbed in thinking about an argument, work issue, or something someone said—even me. If I was not present in the moment with her and instead looking down at my phone, Annie would nudge me so that I was walking backward until I would fall over something behind me. I would laugh, get back up, put my phone away, and say, "Okay, Annie. I hear you!"

Midnight is also incredible at diffusing negative energy and calming down people and other horses. One day, a new mare arrived at the barn, and you could see by her body language—she was pacing, throwing her head up and down, and snorting—that she was quite agitated, putting out angry, pent-up energy. Midnight was loose in the barn, and he walked over to her stall, standing perfectly still right outside of it. I could feel him sending her calming energy as if to say, "Chill out. It's okay."

She calmed down a little, but she was still agitated. Midnight didn't flinch. He continued to send her calming, positive energy. Each time he sent her energy, she would get calmer and calmer. Finally, she let out a big sigh, released her negative energy completely, put her head down, and started munching on hay. Only then did Midnight turn and walk away. He had listened to her griping and complaining, but instead of arguing, judging, or trying to fix the mare's issues, he simply listened and sent her calming, healing energy until all her anger and frustration was released.

It was an amazing experience to witness, and as I watched, I told myself that this was what I wanted to do: not judge or try to "fix" people but simply listen while sending them healing energy, just like Midnight. To this day, I still make that my utmost priority every day.

Although misery loves company, remember that the goal is not to commiserate and have you both feeling miserable. The goal is to understand without judging, allowing yourself to leave the encounter still feeling light and happy—and hopefully leaving the person you encountered better for having crossed your path.

Assuming you have cleared your own energy, I challenge you to keep your arrows pointing out and not in and see how many facades you can see through—whether they're friends, family, or even strangers—and read their energy. To do this, you'll need to see people for who they are and not the front they put on. That means you'll need to see people—not just look and listen—not just hear.

To help you practice sensing energy, make it a game to people-watch and see what you pick up. Clear your energy and then silently observe strangers in a public setting, such as a restaurant, airport, or park. Look at them with clear eyes and see what you pick up about their energy. Besides literally observing, can you sense their energy like a cloud around them? It's amazing how much people truly reveal by their energy, especially when it is in direct contrast to their words. The more you practice objectively sensing people's energy, the easier it will become.

Remember the Why

Before we walk through the process of how to read other people's energy in the next chapter, I want to remind you *why* we want to read their energy. You should always approach energy reading with the goal of seeing where someone is coming from and what they're going through. This will help you view them with softer, kinder eyes. When you take this approach, you may be able to "interpret" their energy and help them realize what they already subconsciously know is best for them but that their brain and emotions are blocking them from realizing.

The one thing you should never do is offer your opinion. This is extremely important; I cannot stress it enough. Your opinion is irrelevant. It's not your job to "change" or "fix" someone, so let go of your ego. Your goal should be to help them see what their inner self already knows, without your opinion coloring their decision. Observe, understand, and then try to guide them to their own resolution.

You should also be careful to keep your own energy clear while reading others'. Observe and notice their energy but don't take it on yourself. I know that's not easy when it's someone you love and you want to help them. But taking on their energy doesn't actually help. Instead, you should acknowledge their energy and then send them your positive, clear energy.

Think of it like a parent with a scared child. When the child is scared, the parent acknowledges it but then sends soothing energy to the child, and the child calms down. If the parent instead responds with fear or anger, the child's fear becomes more intense, and the child becomes more agitated.

So when you encounter someone feeling something negative—like anger, frustration, or fear—acknowledge their emotions without taking them on, and then send them your calming, positive energy. Don't tell the person why they shouldn't feel that emotion; the bottom line is that *is* how they feel. By sending them your good energy, you help them diffuse their negative energy, and they'll leave the encounter feeling at least a little bit lighter.

———

Chapter 5: Reading Others' Energy

Now we can start the process of reading others' energy. When reading someone's energy, it's pertinent that you act as a translator or interpreter and don't insert or offer your own opinion. Your job is to help the person see what they know internally but have blocked. You don't know what that is, no matter what your ego says. You are simply a vessel for their energy to flow through and back to them.

Always Start by Clearing Your Energy

Thus far, I've spoken about clearing your own energy so you can really tune in and read others' energy. Before we move forward with that concept, let's briefly recap those steps. This may feel repetitive, but it's vital to the process, so I encourage you to avoid the urge to skip ahead.

Do Your Self-Check

When you're ready to start really sensing others' energy, take a moment to center and clear yourself by doing the following:

1. Quiet and clear your mind of all the "clutter" and thoughts.

2. Do the breathing exercise to really exhale and release the negative energy you are holding.

3. Empty your gut of any emotions you are holding.

4. Expand your diameter and point your arrows outward. Really see what is around you. Observe, don't just see. Don't just listen; actually tune in to things. Fine-tune the dial like you would on the radio.

Take five minutes to do this every day—multiple times a day if needed—until it becomes a habit. And definitely do it before you actively try to tune in and read someone's energy.

Be Present in the Moment

The most important requirement for you to read another person's energy is to be present in the moment. Contrary to popular belief, this means you have to stop multitasking and really focus on what you are trying to do.

Unfortunately, these days people are so busy doing so many different things that multitasking has become the current trend. Are you one of those people who multi-tasks all the time and secretly feels this is a strength you possess? The reality is that multitasking is not a strength, and although sometimes it is a necessity, most of the time it is actually a hindrance.

The problem with multitasking is that you're not truly focused on any of the items you're working on; you're just doing the bare minimum of what is needed to get it done. You're completing several things, but none of them are being done to the best of your ability.

When you're talking with someone on the phone while doing something else, you're not fully present and listening to that person. You're not sensing their energy or what they're really trying to say. You're simply hearing them while you both plan your response and continue doing other things. You miss so much!

This doesn't mean you can't enjoy talking with someone on the phone while you're out exercising or doing some mundane tasks. But in those instances you are "chatting" with them instead of actively listening to them, and that's okay. When you truly want to tune in to the person you are talking with, stop everything else and be present in the moment. You'll be amazed at what you pick up.

What Is Your First Impression?

Now you're relaxed, focused, and ready to observe. If you are meeting someone in person, try to approach them in a way that lets you see the person before they see you, and do your best to truly see them before they put on a false smile. Are they smiling, light, and buoyant or frowning and heavy-hearted? How do they carry themselves: slumped and sluggish or bouncy and uplifted? What kind of vibes are they putting out? Notice any sudden changes in their demeanor when they see you. If there's a sudden change, they're likely trying to hide what is really going on.

If you're talking on the phone and don't have the benefit of physical cues, nonverbal cues become even more important. Really listen to the tone of their voice. Does their pitch go up at the end of the sentence? For example, when they say "I'm so excited," does the word *excited* come out at a higher pitch, almost as if they were asking a question? That is often a sign that they're not sure or are trying to convince themselves. Usually, when someone is certain about something, they are emphatic in their intonation, and the word *excited* will come out at an equal or lower pitch than the rest of the sentence.

Five Steps to Help Someone with Conflicting Energy

Sometimes you can tune in and read someone's energy when they're in a good place and simply share that wonderful feeling. But other times you might pick up on a conflict, when their words are in direct conflict with the energy you sense from them. If you feel a conflict in their energy and want to help, you can follow these five steps.

Step One: Feel the Conflict

The first rule is that when you observe a conflict in what someone is saying versus the energy they are putting out, do not challenge them. This will only cause them to get defensive and put up a wall. Instead, acknowledge what they are saying and then start asking leading questions. Don't use yes or no questions, such as "Are you sure?" Ask open-ended questions that will subtly encourage them to think more deeply on the subject.

For example, if someone is telling you about a decision they made that they claim to be so happy about, but you see a conflict in their energy, start by saying, "That sounds wonderful!" *(Acknowledgement.)* "What are you most excited about?" *(Leading question.)*

Step Two: Listen
Observe and genuinely listen. It's important that you don't pry to find out what they're hiding. Instead, simply be available and open. Don't just listen to their words; watch their body language and expressions and listen to their tone of voice. Remember, we want to look beyond the words. What are they not saying?

Do they immediately respond with an exciting aspect of their decision? Do their eyes light up? Is there a big smile on their face? Is their voice tinged with happiness?

If that's the case, it could be that they truly want to do whatever they are discussing. The conflict you are feeling may be from nerves, uncertainty, or a lack of confidence in themselves—or it could be something more serious.

However, if they struggle to find something to be excited about, if their words sound enthusiastic, but their voice and eyes are flat, or if their body gets tense, that's a sure indication that they don't believe internally that this is a good decision.

Step Three: Probe Gently
In both situations, probe a little further. Ask them if there is any downside to their decision or anything they are concerned about.

In the first scenario, where they seem to be truly excited but don't have a specific item that concerns them, point that out and suggest that it could just be nerves and excitement. That realization alone may give them the clearance they need to move confidently forward.

On the other hand, if they do identify a concern, walk them through it. Have them talk through what the worst possible outcome of that concern could be, and then ask them whether they would still want to go through with their decision if that worst-case scenario occurred. By helping them identify the cause of their reluctance or hesitation, they will be in a much better position to make a better, more fulfilling decision.

In the second scenario, ask them if there's any downside to their decision. If they list one, follow up by asking if there are any alternatives they could consider.

Remember, you're not telling them they should or shouldn't do something; in reality, you don't know what's best for them (regardless of what your ego thinks). Rather, you're observing the obvious conflict between their energy and their words and guiding them, using subtle questions that lead to the realization of what they already know internally. You'll be amazed how quickly people respond to this type of positive energy and start really opening up—even strangers.

Step Four: Determine the Negative Feeling Cause

From their responses, try to determine what is causing their negative feelings. Is it because they don't really want to do it, but someone else thinks they should? Are they afraid of letting someone else down?

Don't rush the conversation. Keep taking baby steps

and fully listen to their responses. Guide the conversation according to their responses: If their response is hesitant, delve deeper. If it's happy, they're on the right track.

Step Five: Enjoy Their Joy
By leading with open questions and letting them talk, you'll find that they easily come to their own conclusion on what it is they really want. They'll feel enlightened and free, like you just solved their biggest problem. They'll now know the true direction they want to take, and you'll see it in their body language and energy—relieved, light, happy, and confident. They'll leave thanking you for your wisdom and insight. And you can smile and walk away knowing that it wasn't you; it was simply you guiding them to their inner source. What a gift to give!

The added bonus is that when you focus on really seeing other people's energy, not only are you able to help them, but you're also constantly reinforcing the new non-judgmental traits you're trying to develop in yourself, as helping others requires you to keep your arrows pointed out and not in.

Be Aware of Timing
As with most things in life, timing is everything. It's essential that you be aware and present any time you are reading another person's energy. Be aware of what state the person is in at that moment. You may see a conflict between what they're saying and their energy, but they may not be ready or open to receiving the truth.

When someone wants to confide in you, determine if

they want your input, an ear to listen to them, or simply a hug or similar gesture. Resist the urge to jump in and offer a solution. Sometimes a person just needs to know they've been heard. Be what they need you to be in that moment without judging them for not being ready to receive the truth. Often, you'll find that if you don't push and are open and understanding, they will return to initiate the discussion when they're ready.

I've also often found that when I actively listen without offering my insight or opinion, the person wants those things from me and sometimes even pushes for them.

My friend, Mary, is a perfect example. Mary was frustrated because of a repeated occurrence with her good friend Sue. It seemed that every time she was having a conversation with Sue, and Mary interjected with a question, Sue would yell at her, "Why are you always correcting me?" Mary would try to explain she wasn't trying to correct Sue but rather clarify what she was saying. Yet Sue would still view Mary's questions negatively, and after a few more times of it occurring during the conversation, Sue would explode and yell at Mary.

Mary asked me for advice on how she could change their dynamics so they could have a discussion without it turning into a fight. I pointed out to Mary that this was a good example of Sue's arrows definitely pointing inward and seeing everything as being about her. Even if Mary changed the tone of her questions to ensure they were not in any way offensive, it wouldn't change anything—Sue would still see the situation as being about her and, therefore, view it as a challenge or criticism.

I suggested to Mary that during their next conversation, she should hold off asking any questions and simply listen to Sue. I know in our society we're taught to be "good" listeners by interacting: nodding our heads, uttering confirmations, and asking questions. But in reality, interacting can often backfire, as it keeps you from genuinely listening.

By Mary holding her questions and not interrupting, not only could Sue get out what she was trying to say, but Mary would be actively listening instead of interjecting and planning what she was going to say or ask next. I told her that if Sue noticed her silence and asked, "Why aren't you saying anything," she should smile and respond, "I'm just listening. Go on!"

Then, once Sue had finished and come up for air, I suggested that Mary not immediately say anything but rather see what Sue said next. If she immediately moved to a new topic, it would indicate that she simply needed to vent and wasn't actually looking for Mary's input. But, if Sue paused and asked what Mary thought, then Mary could ask her questions and offer her insight. The difference in this situation is that Sue had now requested Mary's input instead of Mary dumping it on her, so Sue would be much more open to receiving it.

Mary thanked me for the advice and said she'd give it a try.

The next time I crossed paths with Mary, she came running up to me, extremely excited, and told me that she had followed my suggestion and had been amazed by the outcome. She said not only were there no longer any blow-ups in their conversations, but Sue had told her she was a great listener. Plus, not only was Sue now open to receiving feedback from Mary, she was also actually starting to solicit it.

By stepping back, observing, and listening, Mary was now able to determine if Sue needed to vent or if she wanted some input. Mary, having learned how to hold back and genuinely listen, was amazed at how much she now "heard" that she was missing before.

Remember, reading energy takes practice. You might not have success every time when you first start following the steps in this chapter. But if you treat each attempt as a learning experience, you'll soon find that you become more accurate in your reading and more adept in your guidance.

Chapter 6: Hands-On Energy Work

I n this chapter, I'll be talking about some important things to be aware of when doing hands-on energy work. If you're not interested in hands-on work, I still encourage you to read this chapter. You may find there are some suggestions, ideas, and stories here that may help in your everyday interactions.

If you picked up this book because you wanted to learn how to read energy, you've probably heard about or researched different types of hands-on energy work, such as massage therapy or Reiki. There are hundreds of such methodologies that have been learned and shared throughout the ages.

While we're not going to get into specific methodologies, I do want to share several things that are important to keep in mind when working with hands-on energy, regardless of the method. My clients in this chapter are all horses, but the learnings and processes are the same whether you work with humans, horses, or any other creature.

Release Your Negative Energy

First, be aware that you are always transmitting energy to the person or animal you are working on, whether your hands are physically touching them or not. That is why it is crucial you are aware of your own energy—if you aren't aware, you could inadvertently pass your negative energy on to them.

Before laying your hands on any living thing, take an honest review of your own energy. Are you holding negative energy that you haven't or can't process? If you are, you will pass that energy on to the person or animal, which will likely resist by being difficult or putting up a wall to block your energy, and you won't be able to help them.

One of the biggest lessons my horses taught me was how important it is to let go of any negative energy I am carrying, especially if I don't go to the barn until later in the day. If I arrived at the barn still engrossed in what occurred that morning or focused on what I had to do tomorrow, my horses would be agitated and act up. They forced me to release all that negative energy and tension before I stepped foot in the barn, and with that came a huge benefit. When I would return to work or whatever situation had caused the hyper or stressed energy, I would find that I was relaxed and ready to dive back in, while my coworkers were still harboring the negative energy from the day before—which was now affecting everything they did that day.

When you have an appointment to work on a client, before you even get out of the car or step into the room with them, assess your energy. Own it and release it. If there is a reason you can't release it (perhaps it's too overwhelming for you at that moment), then you owe it to your client to cancel and reschedule the session. If you don't, you will not achieve the desired results and may actually cause harm.

Be Open to Exceptions

Once you've cleared your energy and are ready to work with your client, there are a few things you need to be aware of. First, I've always believed there's a place for both science and natural healing methodologies, and that together, they can complement each other to get amazing results. Second, whatever methodology you have trained in, the steps you've been taught are to guide you, not be the "rule" of how you work. Be open to exceptions.

I, unfortunately, have an example of what happens when a well-intentioned, well-trained healer is not open to exceptions. My beloved horse, Midnight, was going through a painful situation, and I couldn't find the source of the problem, so I started using various human angels who were crossing our path, each with their special talent in energy healing, to try to help him. One man was well-renowned for his work with cranial energy, so I invited him to work on Midnight. He was a wonderful person with great energy, and I was excited and open to learning how he could help.

He did the first session on Midnight and was scheduled to return at the end of the week for a second session. After the first session, I put my forehead on Midnight's forehead. I immediately felt nauseous and dizzy, like someone was trying to push me over, and I could tell that Midnight felt out of sorts too. Unsure what caused the intense reaction, I reached out to my mentor and trainer, who we'll call Abby, who had worked with Midnight several times before.

She explained that in cranial and other energy methodologies, it is often taught that all good or proper energy flows clockwise, and when they feel or sense energy going counterclockwise, they are supposed to adjust it. While the *majority* of the time this is correct, both Midnight and Abby were rare exceptions. Their energy naturally flows counterclockwise.

Abby told me a story about working with some highly advanced energy colleagues. She tried to explain her energy exception to them, and they doubted her. To prove her point, she had them send her "corrective" energy, which she blocked and sent back to them. The energy they received practically knocked them over, and they were shocked. They had not been open to the possibility of exceptions because they had not experienced any themselves. The rule was the rule, and that was how they worked.

The cranial energy worker, although well-trained and experienced, had actually done harm to Midnight as opposed to helping him, simply by lacking awareness of exceptions. If he had listened to and felt Midnight's energy and been open, instead of simply working as he was trained, he likely would have sensed the exception.

Always remember that your training is a guide. Be open to exceptions and let what you feel rule over what you've been taught. Your gut will never lie.

Stop Thinking and Start Feeling

I sometimes fall short when it comes to listening to energy. In the next example, I fell victim to thinking about what I had learned instead of listening to what I was feeling. This occurred during a time when I was actively learning about energy work and how to use my energy to help horses while simultaneously picking up from my mentors some effective physical maneuvers.

Years ago, I had the wonderful opportunity to spend two whole days working with horses using hands-on energy. During that time, I successfully helped several horses and was thrilled with the results. Then one horse walked up to me, and I intuitively knew that his pelvis was out.

However, instead of listening to his energy, I found myself thinking about what I had learned and what I should do. I tried using my energy on his butt and pelvis, with no positive results. Then, I tried a few of the hands-on maneuvers I had learned—still no positive resolution. The horse let out a big sigh and moved away. I knew he was still out of alignment and in pain, and I was not willing to accept that outcome, so I shut off my mind, walked up to him, closed my eyes, and followed what I was feeling, which meant putting my hands over the top of his head.

Immediately, without opening my eyes, I knew his pelvis had realigned—and sure enough, when I opened my eyes to look, it had. Later one of my mentors explained to me why releasing the energy in his head had released his pelvis, but at the time, it made no sense to me. But I had learned the lesson: I needed to stop *thinking* about how I should fix an issue and, instead, *feel* where the energy was needed.

I know it can be hard to turn off your thinking and solely feel what is going on, even when you're an experienced healer. An amusing example is when an experienced energy worker came out to work on my horse Chapiro. In turn, I worked with her on how to listen and feel in a manner separate from but in addition to her hands-on knowledge.

As an exercise, I asked her to stop thinking and answer with a gut response of "yes" or "no" while I asked her a series of questions about Chapiro. The first two questions she responded to accurately and quickly from her gut, but on the third question, she responded, "Well—"

I stopped her and said, "You're thinking. Stop thinking and start feeling." We went through this exercise a number of times, and she was amazed at how hard it was to actually stop thinking and just feel.

Remember, it's extremely important that you take the time to clear your head, stop thinking, and start feeling. It may be difficult at first, but it gets easier with practice. You'll be amazed not only at what you receive but also at how off-target you may have been, even though, logically, you should have been correct.

If you're not getting the results you want in a session, stop, turn off your mind, and listen to your gut and what the client (whether human or animal) is telling you. Be sure you're working *with* the client and not doing things *to* the client. Let them talk to you and really listen.

Also, be certain that your intentions are pure in providing healing energy to the client. Regardless of what you think or how you've been trained, don't direct the energy to certain parts of the body. Instead, let the energy flow through you, and let the client respond.

When it comes to horses in particular, licking and chewing, yawning, or giving a big sigh are all signs of acceptance of your energy. But if you're doing too much or are in the wrong location on the horse, he may respond by getting fidgety, trying to move away, or even trying to snap at you. Don't reprimand him for misbehaving; listen and change what you are doing.

Energy is so powerful that often less is more. It may be light hands-on, sometimes an inch away, or sometimes from a distance. Practicing from a distance can be best if your client is nervous, sensitive, or has had a traumatic experience that means they can't process your hands-on energy.

One day at the barn, a mare who had recently given birth to a colt started to colic. When the veterinarian arrived and took the mare out of the stall to work on her, the young colt became frantic at being apart from its mother, even though she was directly on the other side of the stall door. He was so scared that he started thrashing wildly and was either going to hurt himself inside the stall or, worse, attempt to jump out and get seriously hurt.

Knowing it was too dangerous to go in the stall without getting hurt myself, I sent the most calming energy I could directly to him from about ten feet away. Instantly, he froze in place and calmed down. I held that energy until the veterinarian had finished with the mare, at which time she was returned to the stall and both horses relaxed, lowering their heads to munch on hay. Only then did I release the calming energy I was putting out.

Energy is so powerful you can use it without ever

touching the animal or human. Not only is that an amazing concept, but it makes you realize how powerful energy is. It also shows how careful you need to be when you're doing hands-on work; if you can do so much from a distance, think of the power available to you when you're actually working with your hands directly on someone.

Thinking Outside the Box

Now that you're focused on feeling and listening, let's move on to thinking outside the box when you're working hands-on.

Be mindful of cause and effect when evaluating potential issues with a client, whether human or animal. The area that appears to be hurt or lame could, in fact, not be the actual issue but rather a result of something else, like taking on extra weight or redirecting energy to compensate for the area that is the true problem.

As a rider, I've always been able to easily feel every muscle of the horse I'm on, instantly knowing where he was tense, off, or lame, even when it wasn't visible. Before I started learning about energy work, I wasn't aware this was unique and didn't understand why other riders didn't feel and react the same way.

For example, I remember riding one horse and instantly feeling that he wasn't putting full weight on one of his legs, even though from the outside he looked totally fine. I could also feel that his back was tight and braced. Over the next few rides, I worked on releasing the tension in his back. Once released, he became completely lame in the leg that I had previously identified.

The horse was given a few days off, and another rider would ride him until he appeared sound again. Then the same thing happened again: I would feel the "missing" leg, release the back, and wham—he was lame again. It took a while before I realized what was happening, unexpectedly through personal experience.

One day, I hurt my foot and couldn't put much weight on it; however, I had to go into a business meeting where I needed to negotiate and, therefore, present a strong presence to the group. I braced my back to take the brunt of the pain, so I would appear to be walking fine even though I wasn't putting any weight on my foot. Instead, I was putting all the strain on my back.

Bingo! I realized that was what the horse had been doing. He was, in fact, lame in the leg, but the other rider was telling him to go, so he braced his back to take all the weight. This made it look like he was trotting correctly even though he wasn't putting any weight on one leg.

Now that I knew what was happening, we were able to have a massage therapist come out. When she worked on the horse, she was immediately drawn to his knotted back and worked on releasing it, much more than I could with random rides. The next day I was told that the horse was dead lame in the exact leg that I had been pointing out all along.

I felt so bad about his lameness and wondered if I had done the right thing. But when I went to see him, he came running up to me with the now obvious lameness, as happy as could be. It was then I realized that, over the months, he had changed from a sweet and loving horse to being cranky most of the time, which had been caused by the effort to hide the lameness in his leg. It was wonderful to see him so happy, despite the leg. While the horse could no longer be ridden, the story still has a happy ending: he lived out his days happy and free from pain, grazing and playing in the fields with his friends.

Be Aware of Unique Goals

When it comes to thinking outside the box, remember that the goal is not always to fix or resolve the issue. Instead, listen to what is wanted by or important to your client.

Years ago, I was working on a horse that had several issues. He would consistently let me work on all but one of them—he was very protective of that area and refused to let me try to release it. We'll call that the primary issue. I was baffled, but each and every time, he was adamant. It wasn't until later that I realized that all the other issues that he did let me work on were secondary and the result of him bracing or taking on excess weight to avoid putting any pressure on the area of the primary issue. (Sound familiar?)

After much pondering and asking for internal guidance, I realized that the most important thing in this world to this particular horse was not relief from pain but being able to perform for his person. The primary issue was serious, and although it likely could have been released, it would have revealed his injury and likely resulted in him being deemed unable to perform and compete. In this horse's mind, he could handle the pain of the primary issue if that meant continuing to perform. He had allowed me to release the secondary issues to give him some relief, but that's where he wanted me to stop.

If I had ignored what he was telling me and tried to release the primary issue, the pain would lessen, but he wouldn't be able to perform any longer. And not being able to perform for his person would have crushed him. He might hurt a lot less, but he likely would have lost his zest for life.

Although our instinct is to always help and heal, I have learned that you need to listen to the person or horse, as only they know what is best for them. (Remember what we've talked about: Put your ego aside and never force your opinion on to someone.) *This lesson applies not just to those doing hands-on energy work but to all of us who are in any way trying to "help" someone.*

Using Energy Skills on Animals

Although observing verbal and nonverbal cues from whomever you are working on is very important, it's even more critical when working on animals, because animals don't typically have a voice.

With that in mind, let's look at a quick recap of some tips we've talked about and how they apply specifically to animals.

Always ask permission before you lay your hands on any animal.

If possible, don't restrict the animal's movement. They need to be able to move away from your touch.

Don't stick with a preconceived plan of how you are going to work on the animal based on how you were trained. Be open to changing your process based on the reaction of the animal. Every animal is unique.

Don't reprimand them if they become fidgety or irritable; rather, take that as a sign that they are uncomfortable with what you are doing. Try using lighter energy or moving to a different location.

Animals know you are trying to help them, and they know their bodies so much better than we humans know ours! Often, they nudge your body to indicate where they want you to work on with them. It may sound silly, but I'm amazed how often it's accurate!

Don't try to "direct" the energy to where you think it should go. Let the animal receive it and process it where needed.

Remember that animals are much more sensitive to energy than humans and will likely take energy ten times faster and deeper than humans. Less may definitely be more. Sometimes you may even need to have your hands an inch or two away from the animal.

And of course, as I have repeated throughout this book, *listen, listen, listen!*

To Recap

When you're using hands-on energy, whether it be for people or animals, it's important to release any and all negative energy you are holding, stop thinking and start feeling, be open to exceptions, and always think outside the box. It's not about you and what you can do for that person or animal—it's about them.

Taking Energy to a Higher Level

Chapter 7: Make the Most Out of Your Journey

This chapter focuses on the amazing lessons I've learned on my journey to discover who I am, why I'm here, and my true purpose.

You may believe profoundly in life after death. You may be certain this life is all there is. Or you may be searching for confirmation that there is more after life. No matter what your beliefs are about the purpose of life, the existence of the afterlife, or the possibility of connecting with spirits, guides, or loved ones who have passed, my hope is that you can benefit from the stories I'm about to share.

I want to be clear up front that I have no interest in convincing you to believe what I believe, nor do I wish to force my beliefs on you. The goal is not to explain anything specific about the spiritual world or life after death—there are many amazing books and resources available created by people far more experienced and trained in these topics than I.

My goal is simply to share the questions I had, the obstacles I encountered, and the lessons I learned along the way. Some of you may be asking the same questions, and I hope my stories provide you with some insight. Some of you may not agree with the concepts, but I hope you can still benefit from the general ideas and lessons.

Depending on where you are on your own specific journey, you may be just starting to explore the possibility of the existence of or looking for confirmation that there is something more than this life. You may be grieving the loss of a loved one and looking for proof that they are still with you in some way. Or you may already have reached the point where you know there is more, and you are trying to discover your own purpose on this journey.

Whatever phase you are in, I encourage you to explore all the possibilities through whatever methodology works for you, whether that's reading books on the subject, listening to podcasts, taking workshops, attending seminars or webinars, consulting with mediums or psychics, exploring alternative energy work, or simply sharing experiences and information with others on the same quest. Learn as much as you can and open your mind to the possibilities.

A word of caution: Don't get caught up in the process and forget about your journey in the here and now. Once you have the comfort that there is something more beyond this journey, don't devote all your time to obsessively learning more and more. Remember that your time on the other side is infinite, while your time on this side is very, very finite. So please, be present in the current moment and live your life to the fullest by being the best *you* you can be.

Finding Your "Purpose"

The biggest lesson I learned on my journey to find my so-called purpose is that our purpose is not to "do" or "be" something specific. Finding your purpose is the process and the journey, not an end result. Rather than approaching it like a job, career, grand accomplishment, or something meaningful you're supposed to do, understand that your purpose is the culmination of all the small steps on your journey and everything you do in your daily interactions.

Some people believe that they know early in life what their purpose is, but most of us feel that we are constantly in search of it. Yet neither group realizes that our purpose morphs and grows as we have new experiences and learn new lessons. Your current purpose may be different than it was five years ago, and most likely, it will morph into something different five years down the road. So don't fixate on "finding" your purpose—it's a never-ending process. And through that process, you become and evolve into your purpose.

While I personally believe that we are all on individual journeys to learn different lessons specific to us, I also believe that they can all be boiled down to one simple lesson: learning how to be a better you by loving yourself, then ultimately truly seeing and loving all other beings. It starts with loving yourself. And yes, you are worthy of love, just as you are.

The first step to learning this lesson is to stop judging yourself and others. The second step is to be kind to yourself and others. It sounds easy, but it takes a lot of growth, patience, and self-awareness.

Just like timing is everything when it comes to sharing what you've read in another person's energy, timing is everything when it comes to finding your purpose. You may want to know your purpose right here, right now, but you may not be ready. You might need to go through more experiences before you can realize your purpose.

It took me seven years from the time I started actively searching for my purpose before I found my way. If someone had simply told me seven years ago what my purpose was, I wouldn't have understood because I wasn't ready. I had many experiences I needed to go through that would expand my awareness and lead me to where I was meant to be.

These years also taught me that we don't have one single, specific, predefined purpose. We all have many different options and routes we can take on our journey, and each one has the possibility to be as powerful and fulfilling as the others. Yet, as I learned, just because you can do something doesn't mean it's the most satisfying path for you. Always remember, you have choices and options.

Finding My Path

That was an important lesson for me to learn, but you need some context to understand how I came to that revelation, so let me give you a little overview of my journey. In my twenties and thirties, I was living life, free and happy, always on the go. Between work, friends, family, sports, and traveling, it seemed there was never enough time to do it all. Life was a blur, and everyone around me was living the same way, so it seemed quite normal.

Then, an amazing thing happened. Horses came into my life and completely changed everything. I now define everything in my life as before or after horses. Before this demarcation, I wasn't the typical horse-crazy little girl that you would expect. Horses didn't even come into my life until my late thirties, but when they did, they came in with a bang, turning my life around and starting me on a journey I may not have expected but embraced wholeheartedly.

As I hope I've made clear throughout this book, horses are masters of energy and natural healers. The journey they took me on encompassed the magic of energy in everyday life, working with energy to help heal, and reminding me what this journey through the wonderful thing we call life is truly about.

It wasn't just any old horse who first came into my life but an amazing, advanced, wise soul of a horse named Midnight. Over the next twenty years, I would learn so many life-altering lessons from him and my other horses, such as being present in the moment, slowing down to really see life, realizing what is really important, and truly seeing and not judging others. Up until that point, although I could use energy subliminally, I had not started my journey to actively learn what energy is and how it could be used to help others.

Shortly after he came to me, Midnight began to encounter one physical difficulty after another, some scary, even life-threatening, and all extremely unique. But each incident resulted in me reaching out to a new person with their own unique gift, be it a type of energy healing modality, the ability to communicate with animals, or another gift.

Although I didn't realize it at the time, each encounter

broadened my experience, exposing me to many new and different methodologies, abilities, and concepts that previously were outside my belief or comprehension. My only focus was on helping Midnight. Twenty years later, I was able to look back on all I had learned and experienced and understand that Midnight went through all those ailments as a gift to me, to guide me to the very people who could teach me and open my mind and my heart.

As I looked back and took in the enormity of all that I had experienced and learned and how it had changed me completely, I simultaneously and suddenly found myself with more free time than I had had in those two previous decades. It was then I realized I felt strongly that I wanted to find a way to use what I had learned to give back and help others.

That was when I started what I refer to as my "formal" energy training. During my formal training years, I was blessed with several mentors, each of whom taught me the magic of energy and how to use it in different ways to help others. My focus was helping horses, so over the next few years, I read every book I could, attended every seminar, took one-on-one training, and learned from some pretty amazing teachers.

I'll never forget the first time someone called me a healer at the beginning of my training. I was floored and adamantly denied it, because in my mind a healer was someone who did powerful things, putting their hands on people or animals and magically curing them, like in the movies. I, of course, was not even close!

Only later did I realize that we are all healers, each

in our own way, and that there are many, many different ways to help someone heal. It can be through hands-on energy or something as simple as listening and really seeing someone when they need it.

I've also learned that everyone's energy works differently, as does how they work with energy. As I mentioned earlier, I have always been able to feel others' energy. But I also instinctively knew things, such as what a horse needed or where an injury was. Yet I often held back stating what I knew when other professionals, such as the veterinarian or horse chiropractor, were trying to decipher where the issue was. My thinking was, *Who am I to question them when they are the ones with the advanced training and formal knowledge?* But bizarrely enough, my sense of knowing turned out to be correct every time, confirmed only after the professionals took weeks or months to arrive at the same conclusion.

When I first started training with my energy mentor, I discussed this with her. She explained that I was experiencing a process called "direct know," which is when you receive information intuitively. (This is also sometimes referred to as claircognizance.) I was familiar with many gifted people who received information intuitively from those around them or who had passed, but it was generally something they received visibly, audibly, or by sense of smell or taste (clairvoyance, clairaudience, clairsalience, and clairgustance, respectively).

I had never heard of direct know, but when she pointed it out, it all made sense. In all the situations before, I had not thought or tried to form an opinion about what the issue was; I was simply receiving the information as needed. So while I didn't have formal training in horse diagnosis, I was given the gift of knowing to be able to help. I was finally able to accept the information I was receiving as a gift to help others as opposed to thinking it was simply my own judgment and opinion. This was a huge, powerful realization.

You would think that with all I had learned, with the very real success of doing energy work on horses and finally understanding that the information I received through direct know was accurate, I was ready to start working on horses on a regular basis. But no—I kept hemming and hawing and making excuses as to why I couldn't do it.

This procrastination was totally foreign to me because I had a healthy ego and little self-doubt, and things generally came pretty easily to me. The strong hesitation I felt toward moving forward made no sense. I knew I could do it. So what was the problem?

When I discussed my hesitancy with my mentor, she invited me out west for a few days so I could spend my time doing nothing but energy work on horses. Those few days were incredible and beautiful, and the results I achieved blew my mind. On our next call, after I returned home, we were both excited about what we experienced, and she asked, "So now are you ready to go out and start actively doing healing work on horses?" Without missing a beat, I emphatically said, "No!" I couldn't explain it; it made no sense.

After more seminars and seeking out more gifted people to help me move past my block, I finally found the woman who helped me solve my block—in one conversation.

At first, like everyone else, she told me that I simply needed to get my butt out there and stop letting fear get in my way. I explained that I knew it wasn't fear, but I couldn't identify what exactly was holding me back. I gave her my standard list of reasons why I didn't want to start performing the hands-on work.

She listened politely and then replied that while each concern I stated was, in fact, accurate, they were also excuses. And when you find yourself making excuses, you need to stop and figure out why. She said, "Let's pretend you are living in a perfect world where each of the excuses you just referenced was resolved and eliminated. Would you be ready to do the energy work then?"

I immediately responded with an emphatic, "No!" It finally hit me. I realized that hands-on energy sessions were not what I wanted to do. Just because I *could* do it didn't mean I *should* do it. That moment was liberating; for the first time in a few years, I wasn't trying to force myself to become something I didn't really want to be. I felt light and free.

However, that doesn't mean all the training and mentoring went to waste. I realized I was happy at what I call being a "spot healer." Instead of doing long, formal, scheduled sessions, I would do spot healing in specific areas whenever horses or other animals happened to cross my path.

But now that I was free of trying to force myself into a role that wasn't right for me, I was back to the original question: What is my purpose, and how can I give back? Again,

could she tell people to walk away from the very people who need help and understanding the most? I felt like she entirely missed the whole concept of the power of energy and using it for good. I went home shaking my head in disbelief.

And then it was time for my scheduled call with the gifted communicator. Before the call, I tuned in to my guides and asked what I was supposed to "do," and I immediately received back, "Teach." By this point, I had had several people talk to me about teaching, but I always balked, feeling I didn't have anything to teach. Yes, I had learned so much and had so many amazing experiences, but I didn't have a methodology that I could teach, so I dismissed that notion entirely.

But the message that came through on the call was clear. Not only am I supposed to teach; one way for me to do so was to write. Now I really balked, as I didn't consider myself a writer in any way. And besides, what did I have to teach or write about?

Over the next day or two, after putting together the experiences from the three workshops and the call—all of which occurred within a four-month span—I realized that maybe I did have something to teach. I could write about all the various techniques and ideas about energy that I seemed to be sharing with people on a daily basis. Simple, yet powerful.

I decided to sit down at the computer to brainstorm a few bullet points, and I found words pouring out. Those words would become the book you are now reading, written with the hope that it will help you on your own journey.

It took a long time and a lot of searching to get to this point, but I found my own path to using energy to help others. Similar to my work with horses, I am not a teacher in the formal way (i.e., teaching a course or specific methodology), but rather a "spot" teacher. I teach those who cross my path based on whatever that particular person needs at that moment.

Of course, I could have taken a different path, perhaps following what many were telling me was my calling, and performed hands-on energy work. And I may have been successful at it and helped many people and animals. But I believe I would have always felt something was missing and never quite been at peace. By listening to my gut and continuing to search, I continued my nontraditional education until I reached the point where I could share and help many people, who, in turn, may then be able to help others.

You, too, will have multiple paths available to you. But always remember the ultimate goals: listen to your inner self, experience everything, learn as much as you can, give back, and make a difference in a way that feels best to you. Don't rush from A to Z to find your purpose. Understand that the journey itself is the goal, and it's necessary for you to experience and learn many things in order for you to grow into your purpose.

While I will continue to try to be open and aware to everyone around me and offer insight, love, and acknowledgment wherever I can, I hope that now, through this book, I can do that for a few more people whose paths wouldn't otherwise cross with mine. In the end, I believe my purpose was always the same—the way I went about it morphed as I gained more knowledge and had more experiences.

―――――――

Chapter 8: Tips to Find Your Guides and Higher Self

Let me be clear up front: this chapter will not teach you about the wide-ranging realm of guides and the higher self. There are countless resources available to explore these topics in detail. Instead, I will continue as I started and share some insights I learned through my personal experiences.

Listening to Your Guides

When I first started learning about guides, I wanted to connect directly and instantly with my guides. I wanted to know their name and have them tell me exactly what my purpose on this journey is—but it doesn't work like that. I've learned that we each have multiple guides, and they don't need names, nor do you have to "call them in," as they are always beside you. Similarly to feeling energy, it's hard to hear your guides talking when your head is filled with noise, so you need to clear and open yourself before you can hear their guidance.

Although your guides are always with you, protecting and supporting you, they will rarely, if ever, tell you what to do. You always have multiple options and routes to take.

Some routes may be easier and some more fulfilling, but they all have important lessons for you to learn and experience. If you take a longer, harder road, you may learn more or different lessons. Your guides will ensure you have options available and support you regardless of which path you choose.

A small bonus lesson for you: This concept applies to you, too, as you are most likely a guide to someone else, such as a child, partner, sibling, or friend. Learn how to be a good guide from your guides. Although you may want the best and easiest path for those you are guiding, it's not your role to choose for them. Your role is to ensure they see and understand their options and then love and support them regardless of which path they choose.

Take a moment right now to review the paths you have chosen on your journey so far. Have those choices made you happy or miserable? Do you find yourself consistently choosing the same path with the same obstacles, just a different set of circumstances? For example, have you left one relationship where you didn't feel valued only to fall into the same pattern in your next relationship? Remember, you have options, and *you* are making the choices. If you find you are, in fact, following the same negative pattern, make the decision to choose differently.

You are strong, and you are worthy. It's time to learn the lesson that path has been trying to teach you; overcome the obstacle so you can keep growing and move forward. Believe in yourself and say, "I'm not choosing that path again." If you don't make the change, you will continue to choose paths that lead to the same result. And if you don't learn the lesson now, you will keep repeating it until you do. Think about how thrilling it will be to learn the lesson and move forward so you can find new paths and opportunities.

While you're evaluating your path choices, take a look at the people you choose to surround yourself with. Do they value and support you? Or do they reinforce your insecurities? Maybe it's time to make a change and surround yourself with those that support you. They're out there, all around you; you simply need to expand your circle.

How to Connect with Your Higher Self

Besides your guides, your higher self is always available to you. Your higher self is the eternal part of you that, together with your guides, planned this life journey for you with multiple opportunities and challenges of your choosing. Your higher self remembers everything from the other side and is always here, a part of you. Often, when you receive guidance by just knowing or feeling something isn't right or is off, it is coming from your higher self.

I've learned a few ways to connect with your higher self, which you can also think of as tuning in to your inner, intuitive self.

The first way is to ask yourself a yes or no question you want guidance on. The first time you do this, you need to identify what yes and no each feels like when sent by your higher self.

Similar to feeling energy, the first step is to clear your

head of noise and clutter and clear your gut of emotions. Then, take a deep breath and ask yourself, "What does a yes feel like?" Open yourself to every sensation. It may feel like a subtle sway forward or backward, a sudden change in temperature, nausea in your stomach, faint smells—there's no limit to what the sensation can be. Then, do the same for no. For example, you may get a feeling of swaying slightly backward for a yes, and swaying slightly forward or not at all for a no. Or, you may get a light happy feeling in your gut for a yes and nausea for a no.

If you can't identify sensations, try this: Start by making a circle with your pointer finger and thumb on your right hand, and then do the same with your left. Next, loop them together like a figure eight (you'll have to open the fingers on one hand to hook them inside the other). Hold them tight enough that you get some resistance when you try to pull them apart, but not so tight that you're tense. Now clear your head and ask what a yes feels like. Gently try to pull your hands apart. Did they release easily or stay locked? That would be your sign for yes. Do the same for no; you'll likely get the opposite response.

Once you determine what a yes and no answer each feels like, you can ask your higher self a question.

But why does it have to be a yes or no question? Because while neither your guides nor your higher self will ever tell you what to do, they will help you understand if something is good or bad for you. For example, if you're having an allergic reaction but you don't know why, you can ask, "Is it caused by something I'm eating?" If you get a no, you can continue asking questions. "Is it caused by something I put on my body?" Keep asking until you find the root cause. Another example is if you were trying to determine which of two items is best for you (it could be two snack options, two vitamins, two lotions, etc.). Hold one and see if you feel a yes or no, and then hold the other.

Once you get an answer, accept it. Don't keep testing it to see if you get the same response. That will get your "thinking" self back in the game when you only want your energetic self. The goal of this exercise is to connect with your higher self, who always knows what's best for you and wants to help. You simply need to listen and trust it.

An important caveat: This exercise is not a Magic 8 Ball. Your question has to be for the highest good and only to get guidance for yourself. Your higher self won't tell you which lottery numbers to choose or give you unnecessary or private information about others. For example, even if you're trying to help someone who is going through a rough time, you won't get answers to personal questions about them or their circumstances, as that is none of your business and not for the highest good. But you will get an answer if you ask if you should reach out to that person. And if you get a yes, you could dig a little deeper. "Should I visit in person?" If no, ask, "Should I call?" If still no, "Should I text?" You can keep going until you are clear on the best way to help.

As with all of the practices in this book, it will take some practice to truly tune in to what your yes and no responses are and to feel confident in your answers. If you feel like you're not hearing anything, check how cluttered your head and gut are. Most likely, you're holding on to something that needs to be released before you can hear. Empty them and try again.

You'll find the more you practice energy work, the clearer you can hear your guides and higher self—and vice versa. The more time you spend listening to your guides and higher self, the more clearly you'll feel and interpret energy. Both will help you help yourself and help others who cross your path.

Anyone Can Be a Guide

I've learned that guides are sometimes hidden in plain sight. Be aware of everyone and everything around you, as you never know where an advanced soul may appear. We tend to judge by appearances and circumstances and that can be so deceiving. I have found some amazing advanced souls in the most unexpected places.

One day, as I was on my way home from the barn, I stopped at a convenience store for a soda. As I pulled into the parking lot, I found it full with only one empty spot— right next to a disheveled man standing next to his beat-up old car with the door open to show it filled to the brim with what many would call junk. I waited patiently for the man to finish what he was doing and close the car door so I could pull in and park. After a few minutes, he looked up, immediately apologized, and closed the door. I pulled in, waved, and thanked him.

While I was inside getting my soda, I heard a voice behind me, apologizing for getting in my way in the parking lot. Without turning around, as I was filling my soda cup, I told him it wasn't a problem as I wasn't in a hurry and I definitely didn't want to hurt him. After I finished filling my cup, I turned around, looked into his eyes, and was stunned silent. I immediately knew he was one of the most advanced souls I had ever encountered. He gave me a huge, beatific smile and, with a twinkle in his all-knowing eyes, said to me, "Have a fantastic rest of your life." He left, leaving me standing there with my jaw agape, filled with wonder. I will never forget the power of that encounter.

Another odd place I unexpectedly found an advanced soul was in an empty field. I was out grazing Chapiro when he started to freak out. He had spotted a huge mule on the other side of the fence. Having never seen a mule myself, I was intrigued. Over the next few days, I slowly moved Chapiro closer and closer until I could reach over the fence to pet the mule. As I gazed into the mule's eyes, I saw a very knowing, wise, and advanced soul, and I felt blessed to be in his presence. Chapiro seemed to sense it as well, and every day after, we would visit the amazing mule together and come back feeling blessed and energized.

I encourage you to keep your eyes, mind, and heart open. Embrace everything and everyone around you, as you never know what you'll find. If you have a closed mind and narrow vision, you will miss so much. It's your choice which path to follow.

Final Thoughts

O pportunities are everywhere, but it's up to you what you do with them. You need to be open to them and take action, not sit around and wait for them to arrive at your door. Try everything. You may have to go through multiple doors before you arrive at your ultimate destination. As you explore every option, pay attention to what lights you up and makes you happy. Don't postpone or avoid trying something now because a better option may come along. Stop waiting and start living!

Remember that, ultimately, life is all about love. It's easy to love your friends, your family, people you like, and those in your inner circle. It's harder to love the ones that push your buttons or who are different or difficult. But it's the ones who are hardest to love that need love the most—and they're also the ones who can help you learn some of the hardest, most fulfilling lessons on your journey. Expand your inner circle to include all those within your reach.

At the end of the journey, you won't be judged by how much you were loved or liked, but by how much *you* loved others, especially the more difficult ones.

A popular saying goes, "I don't want to wait for heaven to change me." I love that saying; it's incredibly empowering. It's often said that when you finish your journey, you review the life you lived and try to see what lessons you could have learned better or where you could have been kinder. I say, why wait until then? Why not do your own review now? Why not change the way you think, feel, and interact to become the better you now? There's no benefit to waiting, and there is incredible value in starting now.

As you embark on your energy-work journey, I encourage you to keep this saying in mind: "Take your observations and turn them on yourself." Remember to keep your gaze on yourself and how you can continue to grow and learn instead of focusing on how others should change. Something that comes easily to you may be extremely difficult for someone else. Instead of judging them for not possessing the strength or confidence that you do, try to imagine how you would feel if you didn't possess that ability. How would you view yourself and move forward in this world? What struggles would you encounter that are completely foreign to you now? Put yourself in their shoes, and imagine living with the limitations or fear that they may encounter every day of their life.

Now that you realize how powerful your energy is, use it wisely and share it freely. You don't have to make all the changes overnight. The first step is to simply be aware of what you're feeling and the effect you have on others. The next step is to decide what you are going to do about it. Will you stay the course, feeling stressed, negative, and out of sorts, constantly judging yourself and others? Or will you expand your vision and make changes in yourself, allowing you to become a happier, more fulfilled person who, in turn, can truly help others? The choice is yours!

If you have any questions about the things you've read in this book, or if you simply want to share a story of how you helped someone by reading their energy, you can contact me at medianoxpublishing@gmail.com.

———

Printed in the USA
CPSIA information can be obtained
at www.ICGtesting.com
CBHW050550011124
16733CB00025B/1035

9 798218 503512